SNAPSHOTS
Silent Thoughts in Words

TAHIRA A. AHMAD

ARCHWAY
PUBLISHING

Archway Publishing books may be ordered through booksellers or by contacting:

Archway Publishing
1663 Liberty Drive
Bloomington, IN 47403
www.archwaypublishing.com
1 (888) 242-5904

Because of the dynamic nature of the Internet, any web addresses or links contained in this book may have changed since publication and may no longer be valid. The views expressed in this work are solely those of the author and do not necessarily reflect the views of the publisher, and the publisher hereby disclaims any responsibility for them.

Any people depicted in stock imagery provided by Thinkstock are models, and such images are being used for illustrative purposes only. Certain stock imagery © Thinkstock.

ISBN: 978-1-4808-5815-2 (sc)
ISBN: 978-1-4808-5816-9 (e)

Library of Congress Control Number: 2018901244

Print information available on the last page.

Archway Publishing rev. date: 02/08/2018

Contents

A Prayer for my Mother

A short prayer for my mother
as she watches over me and
another
walking along beside us
with caring hands and playful
ways.

A quick prayer for my mother
as she smiles down at me and
another,
a baby or a
brother.

A final prayer for my sweet
mother
as she touches us with love on
her fingertips
love that won't lose its grip within
our hearts.

Let the Good times Roll

Oddities in life
Dark matters and a freak show's
wife
Quizzes, brain games and
outrageous acts,
silent thinkers
Mythbusters and all their
facts
Let the good times roll.

The poet and a Ballerina
beautiful words and a
balance beam

Deep down in the woods
a cottage welcomes you
as your world evolves like a
dream
Let the good times roll.

As a father picks up his
baby
a mother's silent prayer keeps hope
alive
Let the good times roll.

On the stage
as we go by
a dedication to time
exposes who we really are
Lights camera and a
Page.

A Prayer for my Father

How strange it feels
the thought of letting go
so harder than it should be
even when I try not to let it show.

I've got to think up bigger
things
I've got to pick up the phone when it
Rings

Playing the blame
game
passing out no
blame
acknowledging all that
came
ignoring all the
Pain

Fond memories may help me let go
after a prayer or
two
or a visit from a friend in
blue
a baby, a mother and a pair of
Shoe

How strange it feels
forever coming so
soon,
exposing the
moon
and a
Sand dune

Finally let's
croon
like a
tycoon
by the
lagoon
Ignoring the impending
Monsoon

Animal Feelings

Body languages and
sounds
mysterious fuzzy feelings and
frowns.
Emotional and feeling
bad
a dog slumps over and feels
Sad.

Instinctive fear in a
Gorilla
defensive pride of a Lion
somewhere in
Manilla.

The Wolf's aggression
a Dog's devotion.

Hackles raised,
fangs exposed
nothing short of an animal's feeling
disposed.

The Home Of Plenty

A happiness inducing home of
plenty,
children playing around and looking
trendy,
homework, bedtime, scarcely
any
even a big hug from granny
won't cost you a
penny,
Seventeen, eighteen, nineteen and
twenty,
all good things here are ten a
penny.
Picture books, coloring pages all too
many.
No one needs to wonder why this is the home of
plenty.

Happy Connections

Feeling connected
accepting disconnections
learning about liberation.
helpful habits and unanswered
questions.

All the mood
swings
creating intense feelings with
wings.

Catching a breather
while renewing your strength.
Gratitude blooming
Happy connections
brewing.

Who am I ?

I am you in all the countless ways that
makes you who you
are
You alone in all your darkest
fears
and all your happiest
moments.

I am you whenever you play the
sister or a best friend's
role
I am you in the secret corner
with a big ice cream
bowl,
any countless
way
even when you
Pray.

Devotion

The present
though a fleeting
moment
has established our
passion,
fulfilled
ambition.

We have made a
choice
with the loudest
voice
just this once
no other devotion will
follow
except when the sun turns
yellow.
Time has stopped for us to be forever
mellow.

The Closet

A closet filled with things that
rhyme
all piled up to save us
time.

Everything that we may
share
from anything that shows how much we
care.
Choosing the perfect
rhyme
let's pass through
time
and commit no
crime.

With a
mime
and a
dime
our closet is truly filled with
things that
rhyme.

My Thinking Corner

A sigh,
a thought
some words
sentences forming up in my
head,
above my
bed.

My life, my friends
hopes and fears
dreamy wishes dangling above my
bed.

A cottage in the woods
the shallow flowing stream where we
stood.

My thinking corner,
a deep sense of honor
one happy learner.

The Stranger

Today i helped out a stranger in
distress
not going out of her way to
confess
the reason why her dog
barks out so
loud.

Sunny skies and a rain
cloud
stranger in
distress,
hoping for
success.

Graphic images from the
past,
making up dreams so
fast.
A sound
a minute
and an hour.
A raindrop
a flower
and a shower.
A transformed stranger with so much
power.

The Earth - Like A Home

We can make the earth our
home
we can create a
dome
and the earth shall be treated nicely
like all other creatures do.

We can make the earth our
home
we can send out a
drone
to inspect all things
Blown.

We can treat the earth with
love
celebrate world peace day with a
Dove
and just maybe
we can learn one or two things
from the lovely old lady and her blue
glove .

The stillness of the
lake
the grandeur of the mountains
the whisper of the desert
the beautiful colors of the skies
all letting us know we're being
watched
by mighty things we can't
Dodge.

We can make the earth our
home
something more than a cheese game
with limited moves
and maybe
just in time
We can build a cocoon of
togetherness.

The List

Do this
do that
do everything right.

Go here
go there
Go everywhere without
fear.

Inspire others
create wonders
seek what is
relevant
a cat a dog and an
elephant.

Establish a bond
explore a pond
sisters, brothers and
mothers...

Think big
go fast
celebrate
accommodate
bring in the jolly old lady and her
purple wig.

Believe in
me
believe in
you
create a
Clue.

Make up a world of
dreams
with everything but
screams
where everyone
wins.

Trackbacks

Earth day and edible
things
climate change and all it
brings
renewable feelings and fearless
dealings,
to seek
to explore
and
rebuild.

Science, essence and questions.
To create
rearrange and to
weed.
Creative actions depicting no
Greed.

Positive thoughts
happy mothers going home with their
tots.
The sky the moon and the
stars
a lion a fish and grizzly
bears.
A Mosque a Church and a
School
a sense of awe that shows no one is really a
fool.

Inspiration (A Beautiful Soul)

I seek inspiration from all things good or
bad
near or far
making me happy
or occasionally
Sad.

A beautiful soul living on the
moon
Red roses and a silver
Spoon

That blissful moment of extreme
joy
sweet little children playing with homemade
toys

Goal setting for a specific
purpose
Birthday parties and all things
gorgeous.

Red green and
blue
Pictures puzzles and a
clue
a castle a house and a
home
an ancient tower with a
dome
I seek inspiration from all things I
See
A Stingray a battleship and the
sea.

Poetic Feelings

Emotions recollected,
like words
recreated
a struggle from
darkness
towards what could be
recommended.

An overflow of
feelings
something spontaneous in all my
dealings
a sigh and i could be
willing
to create a scream out of a
feeling.

Some realization of an
ideal
identification of what could be
real
emotions created in a state of
tranquil.

Night and Day

The beautiful imagery of the
night
seeking out the
day
in a creative
way
each protecting the other
in turn
showing a mutual
bond.

A personal
touch
as someone will always
watch
very evident in an old man's
touch.

The creation of day and
night
depicts all things that should be
right.

Awakening

Consciousness of being
seeing
and
learning.
An accelerated transformation
divine transmutation
total realization
renouncing abysmal
ignorance
exposing the real
significance.

The end of illusional perceptions and
thinking
impractical ideas and dysfunctional
wishing.

Knowledge is
unfold
history to be
told
innate abilities to
behold.

The truth and identifications
awareness of all that is
cosmic
reality and not
comic.

Unrestricted functions
wisdom guided
expressions.
Life is timeless
practical and adaptable.

To learn
to be expressive
to demonstrate noble qualities.

The liberation from
illusions,
the end of troubles and
limitations.
Awakening with endless
possibilities
exploring with joyful
thanksgivings.

Feelings make us Real

How real can we be if all we are is
us ?
on a blue
bus
or covered in
dust.
Feelings make us
real
which erases any need to make a
deal.

We composed a poem
we dug deep down to search for things
we could not even keep.

The me
the you
the us and then
them,
Memories, thoughts and one priceless
gem.
A father,
his baby
a brother
and his
toddler.

Under the sea
above the azure sky,a silent praying
mother
and her smiling
daughter.

A fabric of silk
a small golden spoon,
breakfast as simple as
cold cereal and milk.

A horror movie
all groovy and spooky
another way of seeking out
alternate beauty.

Reboot like a Robot

An Abstract thought
like an autobot
from the planet
Cybertrot.

Like a robot, reboot
Like a robot
compute.
Recharge your energy
do away with an
allergy.

Explore
adore
be bold
be beautiful
it's your show
go ahead and seek all it
holds

Tap your hidden
resources
discover your innate
abilities.

Life can be timeless
humans can be ageless
show you're priceless
be fearless.

Immagine a diverse universe
where everyone can
converse
and
no one wants to
reverse.

Walking the Earth

Walking the earth in lonely
strides
slowly silently like a searching
bride
north and south i searched and
found
a humble man
who's ever ready to share a
pound.
With faster strides and
a brighter
gleam,
I moved like a fish in a golden
stream.
Caught up in one world like a
genie,
we built our home without a
penny.

For all Little Girls and Boys

There's one thing about you that's so
special.
There's something that's so
essential,
when you talk
when you walk
when you sing
when you blink
when you giggle
and when you babble
when you go
bananas
and give endless hugs to your
mamas.

Everything about all little girls and
boys
just so much more than a thousand
toys.

Happy People Stargazing

Happy people stargazing
Happy people soul-searching
which of the stars belongs to
you
which of the stars belongs to
me ?

Happy people stargazing
happy people tap dancing
all the stars
falling out of the
skies
on dark quiet wintry
nights.

Happy people stargazing
happy people time-traveling,
dreaming,
wondering over the
hills,
finally settling down between their
sheets.

Dream Maker

Dream-maker
like my
toy-maker
hops around just like a wish
taker
or a deal
maker.

Where's the homemaker
who once lived with a
Shoemaker,
Didn't she once had a fight with the
Law-maker
Who was not a
Peace-maker ?

Why dream-maker
Did you ignore the
Note-taker,
who surprised the
Drug-makers
with some ideas from the
Policy-makers?.
Dream-maker,
Trailblazer,
everything in between but certainly not a
Mischief maker .

Black Holes

Black holes
dark bowls
Space mystery
Planetary history
Planets or stars
Black holes are
invisible
though admissible
could also be
incredible.

An area in space with very strong
gravity
but no humanity
or
insanity.

Girls and Boys who Rocked our World

Girls and boys who did all things
wrong
girls and boys who were so
strong
girls and boys who tapped on our
windows
girls and boys who knocked on our
doors
girls and boys who cried to be
understood
girls and boys who sought
Brotherhood.

Someone's brother
not a monster
someone's sister
not a gangster
someone's best friend
who'd never pretend
girls and boys we may never
forget.

At the End of my Street

At the end of my street
I counted rain drops
slowly,eagerly as they dropped
one, two, three and
four,
one lazy brown cat at my
door.
Raindrops on my
feet
raindrops on my
sheet
Raindrops on my silly
cat
chasing after his
treat.

A Wish

A wish
to see no one suffer
even as they differ
not even you and I
a big wish
the creator's will.

To fill every room with
laughter
not necessarily in
Winter
a noble man's desire
as he
aspires
a good deed
the very best
indeed.

Two Souls

Two souls found
each other
for the sake of
one another
whoever wishes can go ahead and
bother.

Two souls and a different
mother
two souls found each other
almost on a cold morning, noon or
night,
everything was
right
perhaps not so
quickly
but certainly quietly
could be
inaudibly.

Two souls clicked and took a
chance,
almost without a
glance,
which could have caused the forbidden
dance.

Like One more Time

One more time
and truly the last
I'll defend
wholeheartedly
extend
all that has renewed my
strength
with every single
breath.

One more time
which certainly is the
last
I'll pray for the
best
good things from the
West
everything i'll forever
cherish
memories that will never
perish.

Sending Flowers

Sending flowers of
joy
which may not necessarily be from a
boy
sending flowers to erase
sorrow
not necessarily for
tomorrow
sending flowers to diffuse
anger
if it is ever possible, i
wonder ?
sending flowers to ease
pain,
do they grow in the
rain ?

Like a Happy Hippie

The golden light of the
truth
shall shadow us Like a
Silhouette
protecting us like a mini
Corvette.

We can not be happy
If we stay too long
unless we've been
hung.

Watching our findings disappear
going back to our
void,
let us fast ascend
since our search for eachother
is over.
Let us stay
happy
and live life like a cheerful
hippie.

A Lonely Soul

I walked down a lonely
road
asking for
nothing
because i knew
something.

I walked alone
down the lonely road
wondering if anyone knew
why folks walk
alone.

I met a lonely
soul
down by the lonely road
he asked for
companionship
to build up a
relationship.

Down the lonely
road
I fell in love
with a lonely soul
and flew away with him
like a soulful
Dove.

In Your Brown Eyes

In your brown eyes
so clear and
beautiful
I saw all my dreams looking real and
attainable.
In your clear brown eyes
I saw again and again
nature in full bloom.

The white of the mountains
blue of the seas
Green of the meadows
solitary bliss of (the) dawn
harmony of friendships
variations in relationships.

In your clear brown eyes
true love is
beaming
cheerfully my heart is
singing.

Black and White

Behind everything black or
White
Lies what only the hearts can
see.
Unlike curly waves and the
Sea
Black and white depicts only what eyes can
see.
Painting graphic pictures
we become Black or
White
until our experiences decide what is
Right.

When our hearts desire
Brotherhood
And we see the need to extend our
Neighborhood
colors unite to show our
might
which takes us to the highest
heights.

Images

Images into the mind
instant like a
Snapshot
Into the mind and soul
For the brain to
Rewind.

Keeping hope alive can never be a
mystery
unlike bad deals and mistakes
too bad they're now all
History.

Sweet memories and lots of
fun
feeling so much love for
Everyone.

Special seasons
rare moments,
images can give the truth another
life,
like a crazy man still loving his
Wife.

Images connect dreams
hard as it seems,
even where there are no
reasons
images may rhyme and
synchronize
throughout all
seasons.